First Fish Morning.

Second Fish Morning.

Third

First Fish Morning

Fourth Fish Morning.

Third Fish Morning.

First Fish Morning.

Second Fish Morning.

Fourth Fish What's new?

First Fish Not much.

Fifth and Sixth Fish Morning.

The Others Morning, morning, morning.

First Fish Frank was just asking what's new.

Fifth Fish Was he?

First Fish Yeah. Uh huh. . . .

Third Fish Hey, look. Howard's being eaten.

Second Fish Is he?

They move forward to watch a waiter serving a large grilled fish to a large man.

Second Fish Makes you think doesn't it?

Fourth Fish I mean . . . what's it all about?

Fifth Fish Beats me.

BOOK DESIGNED BY JAMES CAMPUS
STILLS PHOTOGRAPHY BY DAVID APPLEBY

ANIMATION PAGES DESIGNED BY KATE HEPBURN
ADDITIONAL STILLS PHOTOGRAPHY BY CLIVE COOTE AND STRAT MASTORIS
STUDIO ASSISTANCE FROM BRIDGET TISDALL

MONTY PYTHON'S

THE MEANING OF LIFE

WRITTEN AND PERFORMED BY

**GRAHAM CHAPMAN JOHN CLEESE TERRY GILLIAM ERIC IDLE
TERRY JONES MICHAEL PALIN**

DIRECTED BY TERRY JONES
ANIMATION AND SPECIAL SEQUENCES BY TERRY GILLIAM
PRODUCED BY JOHN GOLDSTONE

METHUEN

Why are we here, what is life all about?
Is God really real, or is there some doubt?
Well tonight we're going to sort it all out,
For tonight it's the Meaning of Life.

What's the point of all these hoax?
Is it the chicken and egg time, are we just yolks?
Or perhaps we're just one of God's little jokes,
Well ça c'est the Meaning of Life.

Is life just a game where we make up the rules
While we're searching for something to say
Or are we just simply spiralling coils
Of self-replicating DNA?

What is life? What is our fate?
Is there Heaven and Hell? Do we reincarnate?
Is mankind evolving or is it too late?
Well tonight here's the Meaning of Life.

For millions this life is a sad vale of tears
Sitting round with really nothing to say
While scientists say we're just simply spiralling coils
Of self-replicating DNA.

So just why, why are we here?
And just what, what, what, what do we fear?
Well ce soir, for a change, it will all be made clear,
For this is the Meaning of Life – c'est le sens de la vie –
This is the Meaning of Life.

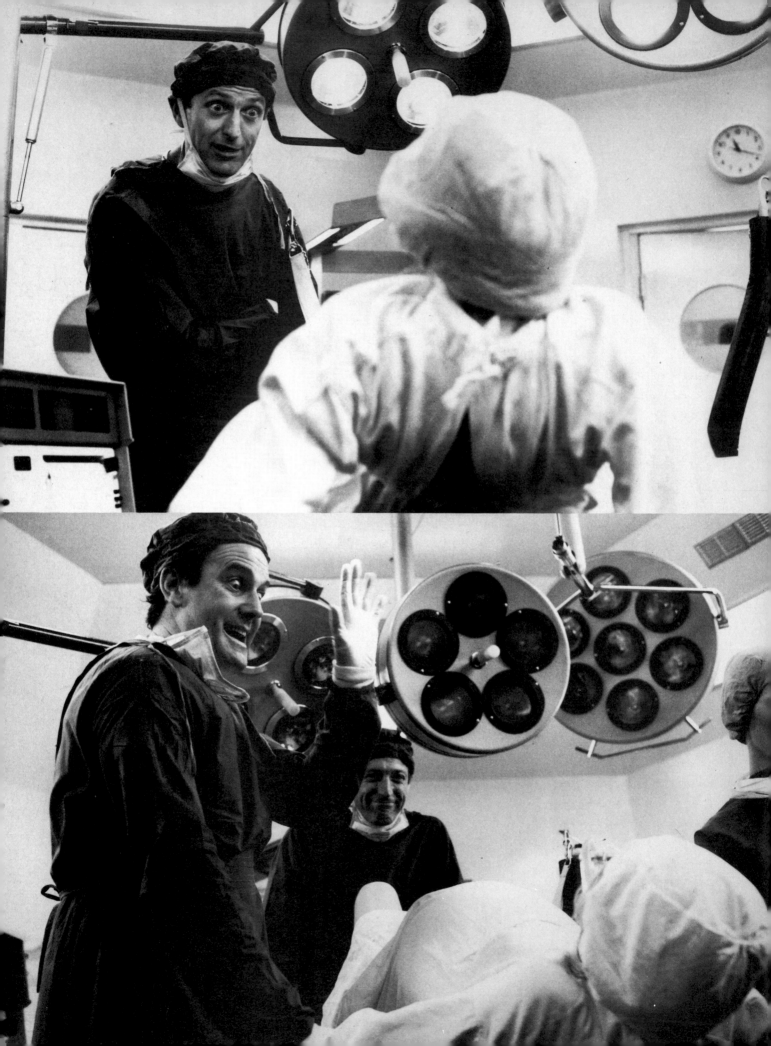

THE MEANING OF LIFE

PART I
THE MIRACLE OF BIRTH

Hospital corridor. A mother-to-be is being wheeled very fast down the corridor on a trolley, which crashes through several sets of doors. A nurse with her slips into a consultant's room, where one doctor is throwing beer mats through the crooked arm of another.

First Doctor One thousand and eight!

Nurse Mrs Moore's contractions are more frequent, doctor.

First Doctor Good. Take her into the foetus-frightening room.

Nurse Right.

They pass through into the delivery room.

First Doctor Bit bare in here today, isn't it?

Second Doctor Yeees.

First Doctor More apparatus please, nurse.

Nurse Yes doctor.

First Doctor Yes, the EEG, the BP monitor and the AVV, please.

Second Doctor And get the machine that goes 'Ping'!

First Doctor And get the most expensive machines in case the administrator comes.

Apparatus starts pouring into the room. The mother is lost behind various bits of equipment.

First Doctor That's better, that's much much better.

Second Doctor Yeeees. More like it.

First Doctor Still something missing, though. (*They think hard for a few moments.*)

First and Second Doctors Patient?

Second Doctor Where's the patient?

First Doctor Anyone seen the patient?

Second Doctor Patient!

Nurse Ah, here she is.

First Doctor Bring her round.

Second Doctor Mind the machine!

First Doctor Come along!

Second Doctor Jump up there. Hup!

First Doctor Hallo! Now, don't you worry.

Second Doctor We'll soon have you cured.

First Doctor Leave it all to us, you'll never know what hit you.

First and Second Doctors Goodbye, Goodbye! Drips up! Injections.

Second Doctor Can I put the tube in the baby's head?

First Doctor Only if I can do the epesiotomy.

Second Doctor Okay.

First Doctor Now, legs up.

> *The legs are put in the stirrups, while the Doctors open the doors opposite.*

First and Second Doctors Come on. Come on, all of you. That's it, jolly good. Come on. Come on. Spread round there.

> *A small horde enters, largely medical but with two Japanese with cameras and video equipment. The first doctor bumps into a man.*

First Doctor Who are you?

Man I'm the husband.

First Doctor I'm sorry, only people involved are allowed in here.

> *The husband leaves.*

Mrs Moore What do I do?

Second Doctor Yes?

Mrs Moore What do I do?

Second Doctor Nothing dear. You're not qualified.

First Doctor Leave it to us.

Mrs Moore What's that for?

> *She points at a machine.*

First Doctor That's the machine that goes 'Ping'.

> *It goes 'Ping'.*

First Doctor You see. That means your baby is still alive.

Second Doctor And that's the most expensive machine in the whole hospital.

First Doctor Yes, it cost over three quarters of a million pounds.

Second Doctor Aren't you lucky!

Nurse The administrator's here, doctor.

First Doctor Switch everything on!

> *They do so. Everything flashes and beeps and thuds. Enter the Administrator. . . .*

Administrator Morning, gentlemen.

First and Second Doctors Morning Mr Pycroft.

Administrator Very impressive. And what are you doing this morning?

First Doctor It's a birth.

Administrator Ah! And what sort of thing is that?

Second Doctor Well, that's when we take a new baby out of a lady's tummy.

Administrator Wonderful what we can do nowadays. Ah! I see you have the machine that goes 'Ping'. This is my favourite. You see we lease this back from the company we sold it to. That way it comes under the monthly current budget and not the capital account. (*They all applaud.*) Thank you, thank you. We try to do our best. Well, do carry on.

> *He leaves.*

Nurse Oh, the vulva's dilating, doctor.

First Doctor Yes, there's the head. Yes, four centimetres, five, six centimetres. . . .

First and Second Doctors Lights! Amplify the ping machine. Masks up! Suction! Eyes down for a full house! Here it comes!

> *The baby arrives.*

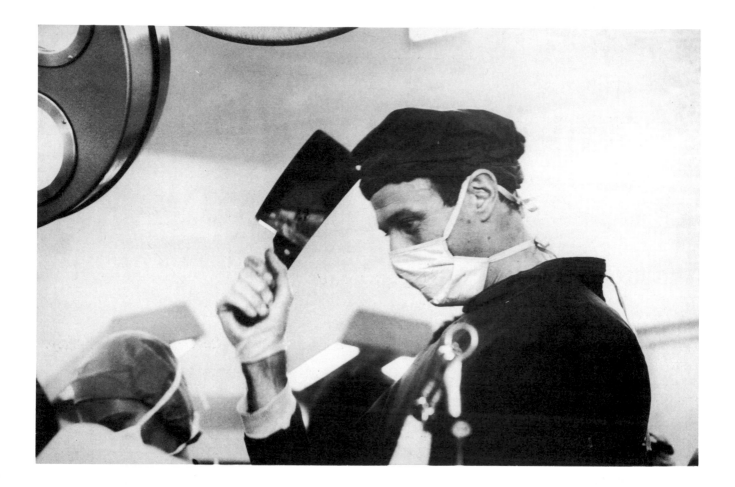

First Doctor And frighten it!

> *They grab the baby, hold it upside down, slap it, poke tubes up its nose, hose it with cold water. Then the baby is placed on a wooden chopping block and the umbilicus severed with a chopper.*

And the rough towels!

> *It is dried with rough towels.*

Show it to the mother.

> *It is shown to the mother.*

First and Second Doctors That's enough! Right. Sedate her, number the child. Measure it, blood type it and . . . *isolate* it.

Nurse OK, show's over.

Mrs Moore Is it a boy or a girl?

First Doctor Now I think it's a little early to start imposing roles on it, don't you? Now a word of advice. You may find that you suffer for some time a totally irrational feeling of depression. PND as we doctors call it. So it's lots of happy pills for you, and you can find out all about the birth when you get home. It's available on Betamax, VHS and Super 8.

THE MIRACLE OF BIRTH
PART 2
THE THIRD WORLD

Yorkshire

A northern street. Dad is marching home. We see his house. A stork flies above it, and drops a baby down the chimney.

Dad Oh bloody hell.

Inside the house. A pregnant woman is at the sink. With a cry a new-born baby, complete with umbilical cord, drops from between her legs onto the floor.

Mother Get that would you, Deirdre. . . .

Girl All right, Mum.

The girl takes the baby. Mum carries on.

Dad comes up to his door and pushes it open sadly. Inside there are at least forty children, of various ages, packed into the living room.

Mum (*with tray*) Whose teatime is it?

Scores of Voices Me, mum . . .

Mum Vincent, Tessa, Valerie, Janine, Martha, Andrew, Thomas, Walter, Pat, Linda, Michael, Evadne, Alice, Dominique and Sasha . . . it's your bedtime!

Children (*all together*) Oh, Mum!

Mum Don't argue . . . Laura, Alfred, Nigel, Annie, Simon, Amanda . . .

Dad Wait . . .

They all listen.

I've got something to tell the whole family.

All stop. . . . A buzz of excitement.

Mum (*to her nearest son*) Quick. . . . go and get the others in, Gordon!

Gordon goes out. Another twenty or so children enter the room. They squash in at the back as best they can.

Dad The mill's closed. There's no more work, we're destitute.

Lots of cries of 'Oh no!' . . . 'Cripes' . . . 'Heck' . . . *from around the room.*

I've got no option but to sell you all for scientific experiments. (*The children protest with heart-rending pleas.*) No no, that's the way it is my loves. . . . Blame the Catholic church for not letting me wear one of those little rubber things. . . . Oh they've done some wonderful things in their time, they've preserved the might and majesty, even mystery of the Church of Rome, the sanctity of the sacrament and the indivisible oneness of the Trinity, but if they'd let me wear one of those little rubber things on the end of my cock we wouldn't be in the mess we are now.

Little Boy Couldn't Mummy have worn some sort of pessary?

Dad Not if we're going to remain members of the fastest growing religion in the world, my boy . . . You see, we believe . . . well, let me put it like this. . . . (*sings*)

There are Jews in the world,
There are Buddhists,
There are Hindus and Mormons and then,
There are those that follow Mohammed,
But I've never been one of them. . . .

I'm a Roman Catholic,
And have been since before I was born,
And the one thing they say about Catholics,
Is they'll take you as soon as you're warm. . . .

You don't have to be a six-footer,
You don't have to have a great brain,
You don't have to have any clothes on –
You're a Catholic the moment Dad came. . . .

Because . . .

Every sperm is sacred,
Every sperm is great,
If a sperm is wasted,
God gets quite irate.

Children	Every sperm is sacred, Every sperm is great, If a sperm is wasted, God gets quite irate.
Child (*solo*)	Let the heathen spill theirs, On the dusty ground, God shall make them pay for, Each sperm that can't be found.
Children	Every sperm is wanted, Every sperm is good, Every sperm is needed, In your neighbourhood.

Mum (*solo*) Hindu, Taoist, Mormon,
Spill theirs just anywhere,
But God loves those who treat thei
Semen with more care.

Men Neighbours (*peering out of toilets*)
Every sperm is sacred,
Every sperm is great,

Women Neighbours (*on wall*)
If a sperm is wasted,

Children God gets quite irate.

Priest (*in church*) Every sperm is sacred,
Bride and Groom Every sperm is good.
Nannies Every sperm is needed,
Cardinals (*in prams*) In your neighbourhood!
Children Every sperm is useful,
        Every sperm is fine,
Funeral Cortège God needs everybody's,
First Mourner Mine!
Lady Mourner And mine!
Corpse And mine!

Nun (*solo*) Though the Pagan spill theirs,
        O'er mountain, hill and plain,
**Various artefacts in a Roman Catholic
Souvenir Shop**
        God shall strike them down for
        Each sperm that's spilt in vain.
Everybody Every sperm is sacred,
        Every sperm is good,
        Every sperm is needed,
        In your neighbourhood.

Even more than everybody, including two fire-eaters, a juggler, a clown at a piano and a stilt-walker riding a bicycle
Every sperm is sacred,
Every sperm is great,
If a sperm is wasted,
God gets quite irate.

> *Everybody cheers (including the fire-eaters, the juggler, the clown at the piano and the stilt-walker riding the bicycle). Fireworks go off, a Chinese dragon is brought on and flags of all nations are unfurled overhead.*
>
> *Back inside.*

Dad So you see my problem, little ones . . . I can't keep you all here any longer.

Shout from the back Speak up!

Dad (*raising his voice*) I can't keep you here any longer . . . God has blessed us so much that I can't afford to feed you any more.

Boy Couldn't you have your balls cut off . . .?

Dad It's not as simple as that Nigel. . . . God knows all. . . . He would see through such a cheap trick. What we do to ourselves, we do to Him. . . .

Voice You could have had them pulled off in an accident?

> *Other voices suggest ways his balls can be removed.*

Dad No . . . no . . . children . . . I know you're trying to help but believe me, my mind's made up. I've given this long and careful thought. And it's medical experiments for the lot of you . . .

The children emerge singing a melancholy reprise of 'Every Sperm is Sacred'.
They are being watched from another Northern house.

Mr Blackitt Look at them, bloody Catholics. Filling the bloody world up with bloody people they can't afford to bloody feed.

Mrs Blackitt What are we dear?

Mr Blackitt Protestant, and fiercely proud of it. . . .

Mrs Blackitt Why do they have so many children. . . .?

Mr Blackitt Because every time they have sexual intercourse they have to have a baby.

Mrs Blackitt But it's the same with us, Harry.

Mr Blackitt What d'you mean . . .?

Mrs Blackitt Well I mean we've got two children and we've had sexual intercourse twice.

Mr Blackitt That's not the point. . . . We *could* have it any time we wanted.

Mrs Blackitt Really?

Mr Blackitt Oh yes. And, what's more, because we don't believe in all that Papist claptrap we can take precautions.

Mrs Blackitt What, you mean lock the door . . .?

Mr Blackitt No no, I mean, because we are members of the Protestant Reformed Church which successfully challenged the autocratic power of the Papacy in the mid-sixteenth century, we can wear little rubber devices to prevent issue.

Mrs Blackitt What do you mean?

Mr Blackitt I could, if I wanted, have sexual intercourse with you . . .

Mrs Blackitt Oh, yes . . . Harry. . . .

Mr Blackitt And by wearing a rubber sheath over my old feller I could ensure that when I came off . . . you would not be impregnated.

Mrs Blackitt Ooh!

Mr Blackitt That's what being a Protestant's all about. That's why it's the church for me. That's why it's the church for anyone who respects the individual and the individual's right to decide for him or herself. When Martin Luther nailed his protest up to the church door in 1517, he may not have realised the full significance of what he was doing. But four hundred years later, thanks to him, my dear, I can wear whatever I want on my John Thomas. And Protestantism doesn't stop at the simple condom. Oh no! I can wear French Ticklers if I want.

Mrs Blackitt You what?

Mr Blackitt French Ticklers . . . Black Mambos . . . Crocodile Ribs . . . Sheaths that are designed not only to protect but also to enhance the stimulation of sexual congress. . . .

Mrs Blackitt Have you got one?

Mr Blackitt Have I got one? Well no . . . But I can go down the road any time I want and walk into Harry's and hold my head up high, and say in a loud steady voice: 'Harry I want you to sell me a *condom*. In fact today I think I'll have a French Tickler, for I am a Protestant . . .'

Mrs Blackitt Well why don't you?

Mr Blackitt But they . . . (*He points at the stream of children still pouring past the house.*) . . . they cannot. Because their church never made the great leap out of the Middle Ages, and the domination of alien episcopal supremacy!

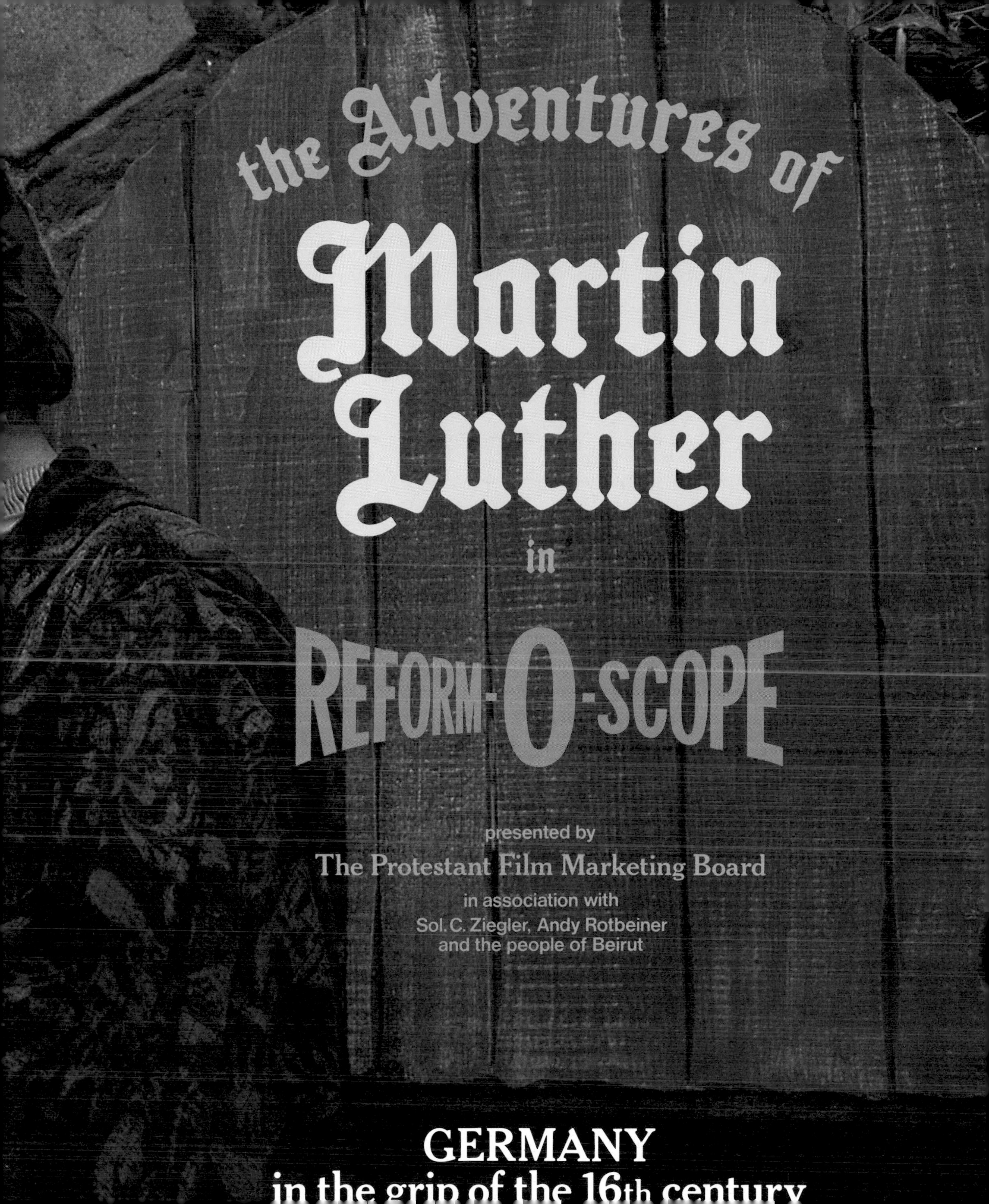

the Adventures of

Martin Luther

in

REFORM-O-SCOPE

presented by

The Protestant Film Marketing Board

in association with

Sol. C. Ziegler, Andy Rotbeiner
and the people of Beirut

GERMANY
in the grip of the 16th century

An exciting and controversial examination of the Protestant reformer whose re-assessment of the role of the individual in Christian belief shook the foundations of a post-feudal Germany in the grip of the sixteenth century.

It was a day much like any other in the quiet little town of Wittenberg. Mamie Meyer was preparing fat for the evening meal when the full force of the Reformation struck.

> *A woman and two rather plain daughters are sitting outside their house with bowls. A man arrives breathless.*

Hymie Mamie! Martin Luther's out!

> *Consternation amongst the womenfolk.*

Mamie Oh! Martin Luther!

> *She hurries her daughters inside.*

Did you get the suet, Hymie?

Hymie Oy vay – the suet I clean forgot!

Mamie The suet you forgot!

Hymie The lard, the fish oil, the butter fat, the dripping, the wool grease I remember . . . (*Hands over the shopping*) . . . but the suet . . . oy vay . . .

Mamie (*pointing to his head*) So what d'you keep up there? Adipose tissue?

Hymie Look out! Here he comes.

> *Mamie goes inside shouting.*

Mamie Girls, girls! Your father forgot the suet!

> *Groans from the girls inside.*

Martin Luther is at the gate. His ears prick up at the female voices. His eyes flick from side to side.

Hymie Hallo Martin.

Martin Luther Where's the john?

Hymie We don't have one.

Martin Luther No john? What d'you do?

Hymie We eat fat.

Martin Luther And that stops you going to the john?

Hymie It's a theory.

Martin Luther Yeah, but does it work?

Hymie We ain't got no john.

Martin Luther Yeah, but d'you need to go?

Hymie You know how it is with theories – some days it's fine . . . maybe one, two . . . three days . . . and then just when it looks like you're ready for to publish . . . (*Expression of resignation and disgust.*) . . . Whoosh! You need a new kitchen floor.

Martin Luther Oh you should be so lucky!

    A girl's laugh from inside. Martin Luther looks up – alert.

Martin Luther D'you need any cleaning inside?

Hymie Oh no . . . today it's all going fine.

Martin Luther Oh well, how's about showing me the cutlery?

Hymie Martin – I got a woman and children in there.

Martin Luther So there's no problem. . . .I just look at a few spoons . . . and . . .

    Martin Luther starts to go in. Hymie stops him.

Hymie I got two girls in there, Martin . . . you know what I mean.

Martin Luther Honest! I don't look at your girls! I don't think about them! There! I put them out of my mind! Their arms, their necks . . . their little legs . . . and bosoms . . . I *wipe* from my mind.

Hymie You just want to see the spoons?

Martin Luther My life! That's what I want to see.

Hymie I know I'm going to regret this.

Martin Luther No, listen! Cutlery is really my thing now. Girls with round breasts is over for me.

Hymie What am I doing? I know what's going to happen.

Martin Luther I'll crouch behind you.

    (*He goes in. Martin Luther follows, crouching.*)

Hymie Mamie! Guess who's come to see us!

Mamie Hymie! Are you out of your mind already? You know how old your daughters are?

Hymie He only wants to see the spoons.

Mamie What you have to bring him into my house for?

Hymie Mamie, he doesn't think about girls any more.

Martin Luther Mrs Meyer – as far as girls is concerned, I shot my wad!

Mamie You shot your *wad*?

Martin Luther Def – in – ately. . . .

    Pause.

Mamie Which spoons you wanna view?

Martin Luther Eh . . . (*shrugs*). . . .I guess the soup spoons . . .

Mamie (*suddenly interested*) Ah! Now they're good spoons.

Martin Luther You got them arranged?

Mamie No, but I could arrange them for you.

Martin Luther Don't put yourself to no bother, Mrs Meyer.

Mamie It's no bother . . . I want for you to see those spoons like I would want to see them myself.

Martin Luther Oh you're too kind, Mrs Meyer . . . You could get your daughters to show me them. . . .

Mamie Hymie get him out of here.

Hymie Mamie, he only said for Myrtle and Audrey to show him the *spoons*.

Mamie Like you think I run some kind of bordello here . . .

Martin Luther Mrs Meyer! How can you say such a thing?

Mamie Listen Martin Luther! I know what you want to do with my girls!

Martin Luther Show me the spoons. . . .

Mamie You want for them to pull up their skirts and then lean over the chair with their legs apart . . .

Hymie Mamie don't get excited. . . .

Mamie I'm getting excited? It's him that's getting excited!

Martin Luther My mind is on the spoons.

Mamie But you can't stop thinking of those little girls over the chairs.

> *Luther is struggling with himself.*

Hymie I got to go to the bathroom.

Mamie (*grabs him*) Hymie! I'm a married woman!

Hymie So . . . just show him the spoons.

> *Hymie goes.*

Mamie And you don't want to put nothing up me?

Martin Luther Mrs Meyer – you read my mind.

Mamie Oh . . .

> *They go out discreetly.*

But despite the efforts of Protestants to promote the idea of sex for pleasure, children continued to multiply everywhere.

THE MEANING OF LIFE

PART II
GROWTH AND LEARNING

A school chapel.

Headmaster And spotteth twice they the camels before the third hour. And so the Midianites went forth to Ram Gilead in Kadesh Bilgemath by Shor Ethra Regalion, to the house of Gash-Bil-Bethuel-Bazda, he who brought the butter dish to Balshazar and the tent peg to the house of Rashomon, and there slew they the goats, yea, and placed they the bits in little pots. Here endeth the lesson.

> *The Headmaster closes the Bible. The Chaplain rises.*

Chaplain Let us praise God. Oh Lord . . .

Congregation Oh Lord . . .

Chaplain Oooh you are so big . . .

Congregation Oooh you are so big . . .

Chaplain So absolutely huge.

Congregation So ab-solutely huge.

Chaplain Gosh, we're all really impressed down here I can tell you.

Congregation Gosh, we're all really impressed down here I can tell you.

Chaplain Forgive us, O Lord, for this our dreadful toadying.

Congregation And barefaced flattery.

Chaplain But you are so strong and, well, just so super.

Congregation Fan-tastic.

Headmaster Amen. Now two boys have been found rubbing linseed oil into the school cormorant. Now some of you may feel that the cormorant does not play an important part in the life of the school but I would remind you that it was presented to us by the Corporation of the town of Sudbury to commemorate Empire Day, when we try to remember the names of all those from the Sudbury area who so gallantly gave their lives to keep China British. So from now on the cormorant is strictly out of bounds. Oh . . . and Jenkins . . . apparently your mother died this morning. (*He turns to the Chaplain.*) Chaplain.

The congregation rises and the Chaplain leads them in singing.

Chaplain and Congregation

Oh Lord, please don't burn us,
Don't grill or toast your flock,
Don't put us on the barbecue,
Or simmer us in stock,
Don't braise or bake or boil us,
Or stir-fry us in a wok . . .

Oh please don't lightly poach us,
Or baste us with hot fat,
Don't fricassee or roast us,
Or boil us in a vat,
And please don't stick thy servants Lord,
In a Rotissomat . . .

A classroom. The boys are sitting quietly studying.

Boy He's coming!

Pandemonium breaks out. The Headmaster walks in.

Headmaster All right, settle down, settle down. (*He puts his papers down.*) Now before I begin the lesson will those of you who are playing in the match this afternoon move your clothes down on to the lower peg immediately after lunch before you write your letter home, if you're not getting your hair cut, unless you've got a younger brother who is going out this weekend as the guest of another boy, in which case collect his note before lunch, put it in your letter after you've had your hair cut, and make sure he moves your clothes down onto the lower peg for you. Now . . .

Wymer Sir?

Headmaster Yes, Wymer?

Wymer My younger brother's going out with Dibble this weekend, sir, but I'm not having my hair cut today sir, so do I move my clothes down or . . .

Headmaster I do wish you'd listen, Wymer, it's perfectly simple. If you're not getting you hair cut, you don't have to move your brother's clothes down to the lower peg, you simply collect his note before lunch after you've done your scripture prep when you've written your letter home before rest, move your own clothes on to the lower peg, greet the visitors, and report to Mr Viney that you've had your chit signed. Now, sex . . . sex, sex, sex, where were we?

Silence from form. A lot of hard thinking of the type indulged in by schoolboys who know they don't know the answer.

Well, had I got as far as the penis entering the vagina?

Pupils Er . . . er . . . no sir. No sir. No we didn't, sir.

Headmaster Well had I done foreplay?

Pupils . . . Yes sir.

Headmaster Well, as we all know about foreplay no doubt you can tell me what the purpose of foreplay is . . . Biggs.

Biggs Don't know, sorry sir.

Headmaster Carter.

Carter Er . . . was it taking your clothes off, sir?

Headmaster And after that?

Wymer Putting them on a lower peg sir?

Headmaster throws a board duster at him and hits him.

Headmaster The purpose of foreplay is to cause the vagina to lubricate so that the penis can penetrate more easily.

Watson Could we have a window open please sir?

Headmaster Yes. . . .Harris will you? . . . And, of course, to cause the man's penis to erect and har . . . den. Now, did I do vaginal juices last week oh do pay attention Wadsworth, I know it's Friday afternoon oh watching the football are you boy – right move over there. I'm warning you I may decide to set an exam this term.

Pupils Oh sir . . .

Headmaster So just listen . . . now did I or did I not do vaginal juices?

Pupils Yes sir.

Headmaster Name two ways of getting them flowing, Watson.

Watson Rubbing the clitoris, sir.

Headmaster What's wrong with a kiss, boy? Hm? Why not start her off with a nice kiss? You don't have to go leaping straight for the clitoris like a bull at a gate. Give her a kiss, boy.

Wymer Suck the nipple, sir.

Headmaster Good. Good. Good, well done, Wymer.

Duckworth Stroking the thighs, sir.

Headmaster Yes, I suppose so.

Another Bite the neck.

Headmaster Good. Nibbling the ear. Kneading the buttocks, and so on and so forth. So we have all these possibilities before we stampede towards the clitoris, Watson.

Watson Yes sir. Sorry sir.

Headmaster All these forms of stimulation can now take place.

> *The Headmaster pulls the bed down.*

. . . And of course tongueing will give you the best idea of how the juices are coming along. (*Calls.*) Helen . . . Now penetration and coitus, that is to say intercourse up to and including orgasm.

> *Mrs Williams has entered.*

Ah hallo, dear.

> *The pupils have shuffled more or less to their feet.*

Do stand up when my wife enters the room, Carter.

Carter Oh sorry, sir. Sorry.

Mrs Williams Humphrey, I hope you don't mind, but I told the Garfields we *would* dine with them tonight.

Headmaster (*starting to disrobe*) Yes, yes, I suppose we must. . . .

Mrs Williams (*taking off her clothes*) I said we'd be there by eight.

Headmaster Well at least it'll give me a reason to wind up the staff meeting.

Mrs Williams Well I know you don't like them but I couldn't make another excuse.

Headmaster (*he's got his shirt off*) Well it's just that I felt – Wymer. This is for your benefit. Will you kindly wake up. I've no intention of going through this all again. (*The boys are no more interested than they were in the last lesson on the Binomial Theorem, though they pretend, as usual.*) Now we'll take the foreplay as read, if you don't mind, dear.

Mrs Williams No of course not, Humphrey.

Headmaster So the man starts by entering, or mounting his good lady wife in the standard way. The penis is now as you will observe more or less fully erect. There we are. Ah that's better. Now . . . Carter.

Carter Yes sir.

Headmaster What is it?

Carter It's an ocarina . . . sir.

Headmaster Bring it up here. The man now starts making thrusting movements with his pelvic area, moving the penis up and down inside the vagina so . . . put it there boy, put it there . . . on the table . . . while the wife maximizes her clitoral stimulation by the shaft of the penis by pushing forward, thank you dear . . . now as sexual excitement mounts . . . what's funny Biggs?

Biggs Oh, nothing sir.

Headmaster Oh do please share your little joke with the rest of us . . . I mean, obviously something frightfully funny's going on . . .

Biggs No, honestly, sir.

Headmaster Well as it's so funny I think you'd better be selected to play for the boys' team in the rugby match against the masters this afternoon.

Biggs (*looks horrified*) Oh no, sir.

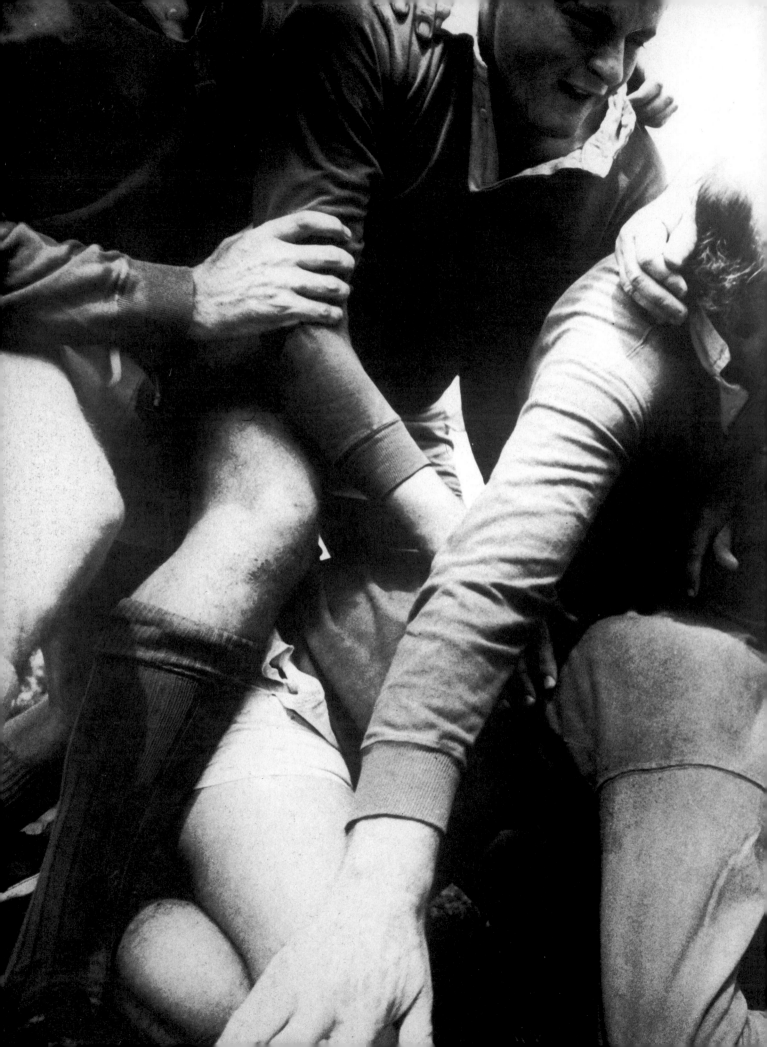

THE MEANING OF LIFE

PART III
FIGHTING EACH OTHER

Biggs (*now a soldier-in-arms*) O.K. Blackitt, Sturridge and Walters you take the buggers on the left flank. Hordern, Spadger and I will go for the gunpost.

Blackitt (*a Deptford Cockney*) Hang on, you'll never make it, sir. . . . Let us come with you . . .

Biggs Do as you're told man.

Blackitt Righto, skipper. (*He starts to go, then stops.*) Oh, sir, sir . . . if we . . . if we don't meet again . . . sir, I'd just like to say it's been a real privilege fighting alongside you, sir. . . .

They are continually ducking as bullets fly past them and shells burst overhead.

Biggs Yes, well I think this is hardly the time or place for a goodbye speech . . . eh . . .

Biggs is clearly anxious to go.

Blackitt No, me and the lads realise that but . . . well . . . we may never meet again, sir, so . . .

Biggs All right, Blackitt, thanks a lot.

Blackitt No just a mo, sir! You see me and the lads had a little whip-round, sir, and we bought you something, sir . . . we bought you this, sir . . .

He produces a handsome ormulu clock from his pack. Biggs is at a loss for words. He is continually ducking.

Biggs Well, I don't know what to say . . . It's a lovely thought . . . thank you . . . thank you *all* . . . but I think we'd better . . . get to cover now . . .

He starts to go.

Blackitt Hang on a tick, sir, we got something else for you as well, sir.

Two of the others emerge from some bushes with a grandfather clock.

Sorry it's another clock, sir . . . only there was a bit of a mix-up. . . . Walters thought *he* was buying the present, and Spadger and I had already got the other one.

Biggs Well it's beautiful . . . they're both beau –

A bullet suddenly shatters the face of the grandfather clock.

. . . But I think we'd better get to cover now, and I'll thank your properly later . . .

Biggs starts to go again but Blackitt hasn't finished.

Blackitt And Corporal Sturridge got this for you as well, sir. He didn't know about the others, sir – it's Swiss.

He hands over a wristwatch.

Biggs Well now that is thoughtful, Sturridge. Good man.

A shell bursts right overhead. Biggs flings himself down into the mud.

Blackitt And there's a card, sir . . . from all of us . . . (*He produces a blood-spattered envelope.*) . . . Sorry about the blood, sir.

Biggs Thank you all.

He pockets it and tries to go on.

Blackitt Squad, three cheers for Captain Biggs. Hip Hip –

All Hooray!

Blackitt Hip Hip –

All Hoor . . .

An almighty burst of machine-gun fire silences most of them . . . Blackitt is hit.

Biggs Blackitt! Blackitt!

Blackitt (*hurt*) Ah! I'll be all right, sir . . . Oh there's just one other thing, sir. Spadge, give him the cheque. . . .

Spadger Oh yeah . . .

Biggs Oh now this is really going too far. . . .

Spadger I don't seem to be able to find it, sir. . . . (*Explosion.*) Er, it'll be in Number Four trench . . . I'll go and get it. (*He starts to crawl off.*)

Biggs (*losing his cool*). Oh! For Christ's sake forget it, man.

The others all look at Biggs after this outburst, as if they can't believe this ingratitude.

Blackitt Oh! Ah!

Spadger You shouldn't have said that, sir. You've hurt his feelings now. . . .

Blackitt Don't mind me, Spadge . . . Toffs is all the same . . . One minute it's all 'please' and 'thank you', the next they'll kick you in the teeth. . . .

Walters Let's not give him the cake. . . .

Biggs I don't want *any* cake. . . .

Spadger Look, Blackitt cooked it specially for you, you bastard.

    They all look at Blackitt rolling in the mud.

Sturridge Yeah, he saved his rations for six weeks.

Biggs I'm sorry, I don't mean to be ungrateful . . .

Blackitt I'll be all right.

    Shell crashes. Blackitt dies.

Spadger Blackie! Blackie! (*He turns on Biggs with tears in his eyes.*) Look at him . . . (*He pulls up the supine form of Blackitt.*) He worked on that cake like no-one else I've ever known. (*He props him in the mud again.*) Some nights it was so cold we could hardly move, but Blackie'd be out there – slicing lemons, mixing the sugar and the almonds . . . I mean you try getting butter melted at fifteen degrees below zero! There's love in that cake . . . (*He picks up Blackitt again.*) This man's love and this man's care and this man's – Aarggh! (*He gets shot.*)

    Biggs runs over to them in horror.

Biggs Oh my Christ!

Sturridge You bastard.

Biggs All right! All right! We will eat the cake. They're right . . . it's too good a cake not to eat. Get the plates and knives, Walters. . . .

Walters Yes, sir . . . how many plates?

Biggs Six.

A shot rings out. Walters drop dead.

Biggs Er . . . no . . . better make it five.

Sturridge Tablecloth, sir . . .?

Biggs Yes, get the tablecloth . . .!

Explosion. Sturridge gets shot.

Biggs No no no, I'll get the tablecloth and you'd better get the gate-leg table, Hordern.

Hordern is shot in the leg.

Hordern (*bravely*). Aah! And the little mats sir?

Biggs Yes, and while you're at it you'd better get a doily.

Hordern I'll bring two sir, in case one gets scrumpled . . .

Suddenly we find this has all been a film, which a General now stops.

General Well, of course, warfare isn't all fun. Right, stop that. It's all very well to laugh at the Military, but when one considers the meaning of life it is a struggle between alternative viewpoints of life itself. And without the ability to defend one's own viewpoint against other perhaps more aggressive ideologies then reasonableness and moderation could quite simply disappear. That is why we'll always need an army and may God strike me down were it to be otherwise.

The Hand of God descends and vaporizes him.

The audience of two old ladies and two kids applauds hesitantly.

Outside the hut RSM Whateverhisnameis is drilling a small squad of recruits.

RSM Don't stand there gawping like you've never seen the Hand of God before. Now! Today we're going to do marching up and down the square. That is unless any of you got anything better to do? Well, anyone got anything they'd rather be doing than marching up and down the square?

      Atkinson puts his hand up.

    Yes? Atkinson? What would you rather be doing, Atkinson?

Atkinson Well to be quite honest, Sarge, I'd rather be at home with the wife and kids.

RSM Would you now?

Atkinson Yes, sarge.

RSM Right off you go. (*Atkinson goes.*) Now, everybody else happy with my little plan of marching up and down the square a bit?

Coles Sarge . . .

RSM Yes?

Coles I've got a book I'd quite like to read . . .

RSM Right! You go read your book then! (*Coles runs off.*) Now everybody else quite content to join in with my little scheme of marching hup and down the square?

Wyclif Sarge?

RSM Yes, Wyclif, what is it?

Wyclif (*tentatively*) Well . . . I'm . . . er . . . learning the piano . . .

RSM (*with contempt*) 'Learning the piano'?

Wyclif Yes, sarge . . .

RSM And I suppose you want to go and practise eh? Marching up and down the square not good enough for you, eh?

Wyclif Well . . .

RSM Right! Off you go! (*Turns to the rest.*) Now what about the rest of you? Rather be at the pictures I suppose.

Squad Ooh, yes, ooh rather.

RSM All right off you go. (*They go.*) Bloody army! I don't know what it's coming to. . . . Right, Sgt Major, marching up and down the square . . . Left-right-left . . . left . . . left . . . left-right-left . . .

    The RSM marches himself off into the distance of the barracks square.

Democracy and humanitarianism have always been trade marks of the British Army and have stamped its triumph throughout history, in the furthest-flung corners of the Empire. But no matter where or when there was fighting to be done, it has always been the calm leadership of the officer class that has made the British Army what it is.

The First Zulu War.
Natal 1879 (not Glasgow)

Inside a tent

Pakenham-Walsh Morning Ainsworth.

Ainsworth Morning Pakenham-Walsh.

Pakenham-Walsh Sleep well?

Ainsworth Not bad. Bitten to shreds though. Must be a hole in the bloody mosquito net.

Pakenham-Walsh Yes, savage little blighters aren't they?

First Lieut Chadwick (*arriving*) Excuse me, sir.

Ainsworth Yes Chadwick?

Chadwick I'm afraid Perkins got rather badly bitten during the night.

Ainsworth Well so did we. Huh.

Chadwick Yes, but I do think doctor ought to see him.

Ainsworth Well go and fetch him, then.

Chadwick Right you are, sir.

Ainsworth Suppose I'd better go along. Coming, Pakenham?

Pakenham-Walsh Yes I suppose so.

> *Chadwick leaves. Ainsworth and Pakenham-Walsh thread their leisurely way through the line of assegais. Pakenham-Walsh's valet is speared by a Zulu warrior but Pakenham-Walsh valiantly saves his jacket from the mud. They enter Perkins's tent. Perkins is on his camp bed.*

Ainsworth Ah! Morning Perkins.

Perkins Morning sir.

Ainsworth What's all the trouble then?

Perkins Bitten sir. During the night.

Ainsworth Hm. Whole leg gone eh?

Perkins Yes.

As they talk, the din of battle continues outside. Screams of dying men, crackling of tents set on fire.

Ainsworth How's it feel?

Perkins Stings a bit.

Ainsworth Mmm. Well it would, wouldn't it. That's quite a bite you've got there you know.

Perkins Yes, real beauty isn't it?

All Yes.

Ainsworth Any idea how it happened?

Perkins None at all. Complete mystery to me. Woke up just now . . . one sock too many.

Pakenham-Walsh You must have a hell of a hole in your net.

Ainsworth Hm. Well we've sent for the doctor.

Perkins Ooh, hardly worth it, is it?

Ainsworth Oh yes . . . better safe than sorry.

Pakenham-Walsh Yes, good Lord, look at this.

He indicates a gigantic hole in the mosquito net.

Ainsworth By jove, that's enormous.

Pakenham-Walsh You don't think it'll come back, do you?

Ainsworth For more, you mean?

Pakenham-Walsh Yes.

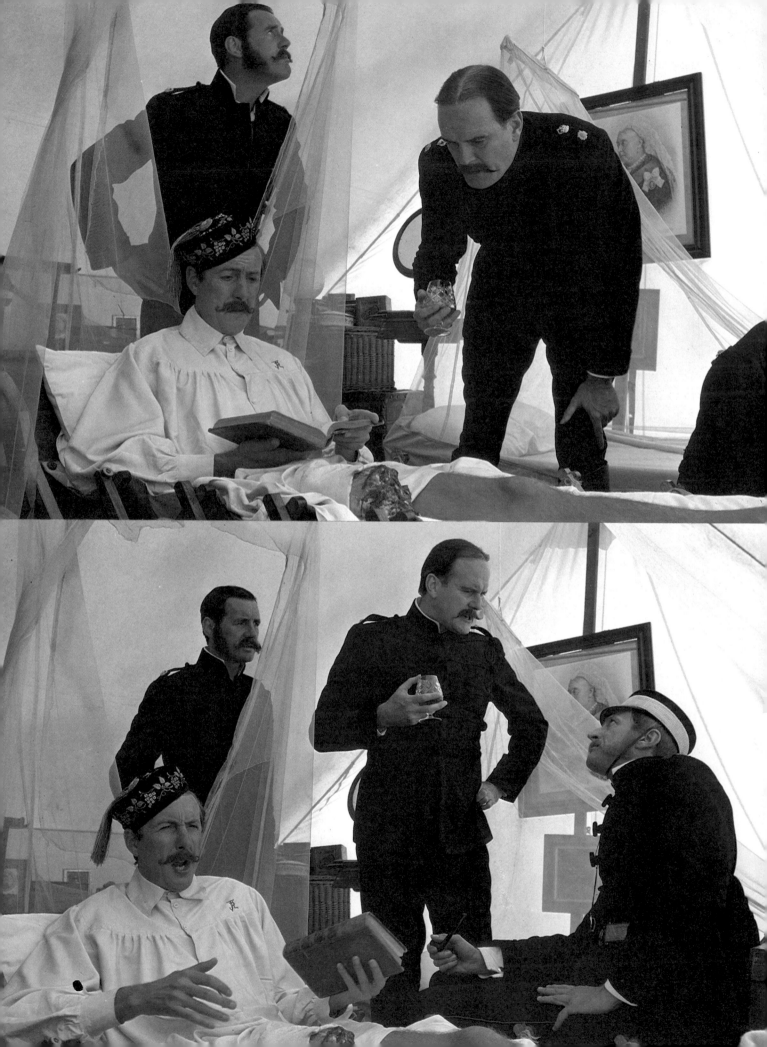

Ainsworth You're right. We'd better get this stitched.

Pakenham-Walsh Right.

Ainsworth Hallo Doc.

Livingstone (*entering the tent with Chadwick*) Morning. I came as fast as I could. Is something up?

Ainsworth Yes, during the night old Perkins had his leg bitten sort of . . . off.

Livingstone Ah hah!? Been in the wars have we?

Perkins Yes.

Livingstone Any headache, bowels all right? Well, let's have a look at this one leg of yours then. (*Looks around under sheet*) Yes . . . yes . . . yes . . . yes . . . yes . . . yes . . . well, this is nothing to worry about.

Perkins Oh good.

Livingstone There's a lot of it about, probably a virus, keep warm, plenty of rest, and if you're playing football or anything try and favour the other leg.

Perkins Oh rightho.

Livingstone Be as right as rain in a couple of days.

Perkins Thanks for the reassurance, doc.

Livingstone Not at all, that's what I'm here for. Any other problems I can reassure you about?

Perkins No I'm fine.

Livingstone Jolly good. Well, must be off.

Perkins So it'll just grow back then, will it?

Livingstone Er. . . . I think I'd better come clean with you about this . . . it's . . . um it's not a virus, I'm afraid. You see, a virus is what we doctors call very very small. So small it could not possibly have made off with a whole leg. What we're looking for here is I think, and this is no more than an educated guess, I'd like to make that clear, is some multi-cellular life form with stripes, huge razor-sharp teeth, about eleven foot long and of the genus *felis horribilis*. What we doctors, in fact, call a tiger.

All in tent A tiger . . . !!

> Outside, everyone engaged in battle, including the Zulus, breaks off and shouts in horror:

All A tiger!

> The Zulus run off.

Pakenham-Walsh A tiger – in Africa?

Ainsworth Hm . . .

Pakenham-Walsh A tiger in Africa . . .?

Ainsworth Ah . . . well it's probably escaped from a zoo.

Pakenham-Walsh Well it doesn't sound very likely.

Ainsworth (*quietly*) Stumm, stumm . . .

> *A severely-wounded Sergeant staggers into the tent.*

Sergeant Sir, sir, the attack's over, sir! The Zulus are retreating.

Ainsworth (*dismissively*) Oh jolly good. (*He turns back to the group around Perkins*)

Sergeant Quite a lot of casualities though, sir. C Division wiped out. Signals gone. Thirty men killed in F Section. I should think about a hundred – a hundred and fifty men altogether.

Ainsworth (*not very interested*) Yes, yes I see, yes . . . Jolly good.

Sergeant I haven't got the final figures, sir. There's a lot of seriously wounded in the compound . . .

Ainsworth (*interrupting*) Yes . . . well, the thing is, Sergeant, I've got a bit of a problem here. (*With gravity.*) One of the officers has lost a leg.

Sergeant (*stunned by the news*) Oh *no,* sir!

Ainsworth (*gravely*) I'm afraid so. Probably a tiger.

Sergeant In Africa?

Ainsworth and Pakenham-Walsh Stumm, stumm . . .

Ainsworth The M.O. says we can stitch it back on if we can find it immediately.

Sergeant Right sir! I'll organise a party right away, sir!

Ainsworth Well it's hardly the time for that, is it Sergeant. . . ?

Sergeant A search party . . .

Ainsworth Ah! *Much* better idea. I'll tell you what, organise one straight away.

Sergeant Yes sir.

> *Outside dead British bodies (of the other ranks) are everywhere.*

Sergeant (*apologetically*) Sorry about the mess, sir. We'll try and get it cleared up, by the time you get back.

> *They walk through the carnage. Orderlies are cheerfully attending to the equally cheery wounded and the only slightly less cheery dead.*

A dying man (*covered in blood*) We showed 'em, didn't we, sir?

Ainsworth Yes.

> *He gives a thumbs up and dies.*

Sergeant (*addressing a soldier who is giving water to a dying man*) We've got to get a search party, leave that alone.

Another cheery cockney (*with an assegai sticking out of his chest*) This is fun, sir, innit . . . all this killing . . . bloodshed . . . bloody good fun sir, innit?

Ainsworth (*abstracted*) Yes . . . very good.

> *He waves and moves on.*

A severed head Morning, sir!

Ainsworth Nasty wound you've got there, Potter.

Severed head (*cheerily*) Thank you very much sir!

Ainsworth Come on private – we're making up a search party.

Another terrible casualty Better than staying at home, eh sir! At home if you kill someone they arrest you. Here they give you a gun, and show you what to do, sir. I mean, I killed fifteen of those buggers sir! Now at home they'd hang me. *Here* they give me a fucking medal sir!

The search party for Perkins's leg is passing through thick jungle. As they emerge into a clearing they suddenly see a tiger's head sticking out of some bushes.

Ainsworth Look!

Their eyes follow along the bushes to where the tiger's tail is sticking out several yards away. For a moment it looks like a very long tiger.

My God, it's *huge!*

The tiger's head rises up out of the thicket with its paws up. The tiger's rear end backs out of the thicket further down.

Rear end Don't shoot . . . don't shoot. We're not a tiger. (*Takes off head.*) We were just . . . um . . .

Ainsworth Why are you dressed as a tiger?

Rear end Hmmm . . . oh . . . why! Why why . . . isn't it a lovely day today . . .?

Ainsworth Answer the question.

Rear end Oh we were just er . . .

Front end Actually! We're dressed like this because . . . oh no that's not it.

Rear end We did it for a lark. Part of a spree. High spirits you know. Simple as that.

Front end Nothing more to it . . .

All stare.

Well *actually* . . . we're on a mission for British Intelligence, there's a pro-Tsarist Ashanti Chief . . .

Rear end No, no.

Front end No, no, no.

Rear end No, no we're doing it for an advertisement . . .

Front end Ah that's it, forget about the Russians. We're doing an advert for Tiger Brand Coffee.

Rear end 'Tiger Brand Coffee is a real treat
Even tigers prefer a cup of it to real meat'.
   Pause.

Ainsworth Now look . . .

Rear end All right, all right. We are dressed as a tiger because he had an auntie who did it in 1839 and this is the fiftieth anniversary.

Front end No. We're doing it for a bet.

Rear end God told us to do it.

Front end To tell the truth, we are completely mad. We are inmates of a Bengali psychiatric institution and we escaped by making this skin out of old used cereal packets . . .

Perkins It doesn't matter.

Ainsworth What?

Perkins It doesn't matter why they're dressed as a tiger, have they got my leg?

Ainsworth Good thinking. Well have you?

Rear end Actually!

Ainsworth Yes.

Rear end It's because we were thinking of training as taxidermists and we wanted to get a feel of it from the animal's point of view.

Ainsworth Be quiet. Now, look we're just asking you if you have got this man's leg. . . .

Front end A wooden leg?

Ainsworth No, no, a proper leg. Look he was fast asleep and someone or something came in and removed it.

Front end Without waking him up?

Ainsworth Yes.

Front end I don't believe you.

Rear end We found the tiger skin in a bicycle shop in Cairo, and the owner wanted it taken down to Dar Es Salaam.

Ainsworth Shut up. Now look, have you or have you not got his leg?

Rear end Yes.

Front end No. No no no.

Both No no no no no no. Nope. No.

Ainsworth Why did you say 'yes'?

Front end I didn't.

Ainsworth I'm not talking to you . . .

Rear end Er . . . er . . .

Ainsworth Right! Search the thicket.

Front end Oh come on, I mean do we look like the sort of chaps who'd creep into a camp at . . . night, steal into someone's tent, anaesthetise them, tissue-type them, amputate a leg and run away with it?

Ainsworth Search the thicket!

Front end Oh *leg*! You're looking for a *leg*. Actually I think there is one in there somewhere. Somebody must have abandoned it here, knowing you were coming after it, and we stumbled across it actually and wondered what it was. . . . They'll be miles away by now and I expect we'll have to take all the blame.

During the last exchange a native turns and leers at the camera, while the dialogue continues behind him. Then he unzips his body to reveal a fully dressed white announcer in dinner jacket and bow tie underneath.

Zulu announcer Hallo, good evening and welcome to the Middle of the Film.

Lady TV presenter Hallo and welcome to the Middle Of The Film. The moment where we take a break and invite you, the audience, to join us, the film-makers, in 'Find The Fish'. We're going to show you a scene from another film and ask you to guess where the fish is. But if you think you know, don't keep it to yourselves – YELL OUT – so that all the cinema can hear you. So here we are with 'Find The Fish'.

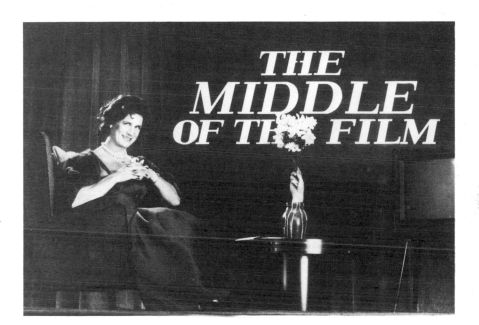

FIND THE FISH

Man	I wonder where that fish has gone.
Woman	You did love it so. You looked after it like a son.
Man (*strangely*)	And it went wherever I did go.
Woman	Is it in the cupboard?
Audience	Yes! No!
Woman	Wouldn't you like to know. It was a lovely little fish.
Man (*strangely*)	And it went wherever I did go.
Man in audience	It's behind the sofa!
	An elephant joins the man and woman.
Woman	Where can the fish be?
Man in audience	Have you thought of the drawers in the bureau?
Woman	It is a most elusive fish.
Man (*strangely*)	And it went wherever I did go!
Woman	Oh fishy, fishy, fishy, fish.
Man	Fish, fish, fish, fishy oh!
Woman	Oh fishy, fishy, fishy fish.
Man (*strangely*)	That went wherever I did go.

HAVE YOU THOUGHT OF THE DRAWERS IN THE BUREAU?

YES!

FIND THE FISH

NO!

IT'S BEHIND THE SOFA!

First fish That was terrific!

Second fish Great!

Third fish Best bit so far.

Fishes Yeah! Absolutely . . .! Terrific! Yeah! . . . Fantastic . . . Really great

Whistles. 'More' . . . Pause.

Fifth fish They haven't said much about the Meaning of Life so far, have they . . .?

First fish Well, it's been building up to it.

Second fish Has it?

Fifth fish Yeah, I expect they'll get on to it now.

Third fish Personally I very much doubt if they're going to say anything about the Meaning of Life at all.

Fourth fish Oh, come on . . . they've got to say something . . .

Other fishes . . . Bound to . . . yeah . . . yeah . . .

They swim around a bit.

Second fish Not much happening at the moment, is there . . .?

THE MEANING OF LIFE

PART IV
MIDDLE AGE

A hotel lobby. The lift doors open.

Mrs Hendy is bending down in front of Mr Hendy, doing something of an intimate nature to his camera lens.

Mr Hendy Oh that's much better. Thank you honey.

Mrs Hendy You're welcome.

Mr Hendy It was all sort of misty before. That's fine.

A strange girl in a crinoline steps forward. This is M'Lady Joeline, played by Mr Gilliam.

Joeline Hi! How are you?

Mr Hendy Oh we're just fine.

Joeline So what kind of food you like to eat this evening?

Mr Hendy Well we sort of like pineapples . . .

Mrs Hendy Yeah, we love pineapple.

Mr Hendy Yeah anything with pineapples in is great for us . . .

Joeline Well, how about the Dungeon Room?

Mr Hendy Oh that sounds fine . . .

Joeline Sure is. It's real Hawaiian food served in an authentic medieval English dungeon
atmosphere . . .

*Suddenly a red hot brand sears the flesh of some poor wretch. This is the restaurant. Dark, full of
torture instruments, stocks, Chamber of Horrors stuff.*

They sit down. A waitress dressed in a grotesque travesty of a Beefeater's outfit, comes up.

Waitress Hello, I'm Diana, I'm your waitress for tonight . . . Where are you from?

Mr and Mrs Hendy We're from Room 259.

Mr Hendy Where are you from?

Waitress (*pointing to kitchen*) Oh I'm from out of those doors over there . . .

Mr Hendy Oh.

Mrs Hendy Great . . .

Waitress (*reaching across to the central serving table*) Iced Water . . .

Mrs Hendy Oh thank you . . .

Waitress Coffee . . .

Mr Hendy Thank you *very* much . . .

Waitress Ketchup . . .

Mr Hendy Oh lovely . . . real nice

Waitress T.V. . . .?

Mr Hendy Oh . . . that's fine . . .

Mrs Hendy Yeah that's swell

        The Waitress dumps a T.V. down on the table.

Waitress Telephone . . .

Mr Hendy Er . . . telephone . . .?

Waitress You can phone any other table in the restaurant after six.

Mr Hendy Oh that's great . . .

Mrs Hendy Some choice . . .

Mr Hendy Yeah, right . . .

Waitress O.K. . . . D'you want any food with your meal?

Mr Hendy Well, what d'you have?

Waitress Well we have things shaped like this in green or we have things shaped like that in brown . . .

Mr Hendy What d'you think darling?

Mrs Hendy Well it *is* our anniversary, Marvin . . .

Mr Hendy Yeah . . . what the hell . . . we'll have a couple of things shaped like that in brown, please . . .

Waitress O.K. fine . . . thank you sir . . . (*She writes*) . . . 2 brown Number 259 . . . and will you be having intercourse tonight . . .?

Mr Hendy Er . . . do we have to decide now . . .?

Mrs Hendy Sounds a good idea honey. I mean it sounds swell. I mean why not?

Mr Hendy Yeah, right . . . could be fun . . .

> *Waitress takes out a condom and slaps it on the table.*

Waitress Compliments of the Super Inn – Have a nice fuck!

Mr Hendy Oh, thank you.

Waitress You're welcome . . .

> *She leaves.*

Mr Hendy (*reads*): 'Super Inn Skins' – that's nice.

> *Suddenly a Hawaiian band comes through the door and surrounds Mr and Mrs Hendy at their table, before leaving them to their own devices, which are not many. There is a long silence.*

Waiter Good evening . . . would you care for something to talk about?

> *He hands them each a menu card with a list of subjects on.*

Mr Hendy Oh that would be wonderful.

Waiter Our special tonight is minorities . . .

Mr Hendy Oh that sounds real interesting . . .

Mrs Hendy What's this conversation here . . .?

Waiter Oh that's football . . . you can talk about the Stealers-Bears game, Saturday . . . or you could reminisce about really great World Series –

Mrs Hendy No . . . no, no.

Mr Hendy What's this one here?

Waiter That's philosophy.

Mrs Hendy Is that a sport?

Waiter No, it's more of an attempt to construct a viable hypothesis to explain the Meaning of Life.

> *The fish in the tank suddenly prick up their fins.*

Fish What's he say, eh?

Mr Hendy Oh that sounds wonderful . . . Would you like to talk about the Meaning of Life, darling . . .?

Mrs Hendy Sure, why not?

Waiter Philosophy for two?

Mr Hendy Right . . .

Waiter You folks want me to start you off?

Mr Hendy Oh really we'd appreciate that . . .

Waiter OK. Well er . . . look, have you ever wondered just why you're here?

Mr Hendy Well . . . we went to Miami last year and California the year before that, and we've . . .

Waiter No, no . . . I mean why *we're* here. On this planet?

Mr Hendy (*guardedly*). . . . N . . . n . . . nope.

Waiter Right! Have you ever *wanted* to know what it's all about?

Mr Hendy (*emphatically*). No!

Waiter Right ho! Well, see, throughout history there have been certain men and women who have tried to find the solution to the mysteries of existence.

Mrs Hendy Great.

Waiter And we call these guys 'philosophers'.

Mrs Hendy And that's what we're talking about!

Waiter Right!

Mrs Hendy That's neat!

Waiter Well you look like you're getting the idea, so why don't I give you these conversation cards – they'll tell you a little about philosophical method, names of famous philosophers . . . there y'are. Have a nice conversation!

Mr Hendy Thank you! Thank you very much.

     He leaves.

Mrs Hendy He's cute.

Mr Hendy Yeah, real understanding.

     They sit and look at the cards, then rather formally and uncertainly Mrs Hendy opens the conversation.

Mrs Hendy Oh! I never knew *Schopenhauer* was a *philosopher* . . .

Mr Hendy Oh yeah . . . He's the one that begins with an S.

Mrs Hendy Oh . . .

Mr Hendy . . . Um (*pause*) . . . like Nietzsche . . .

Mrs Hendy Does Nietzsche being with an S?

Mr Hendy There's an S in Nietzsche . . .

Mrs Hendy Oh wow! Yes there is. Do all philosophers have an S in them?

Mr Hendy Yeah I think most of them do.

Mrs Hendy Oh! . . . Does that mean Selina Jones is a philosopher?

Mr Hendy Yeah . . . Right, she could be . . . she sings about the Meaning of Life.

Mrs Hendy Yeah, that's right, but I don't think she writes her own material.

Mr Hendy No. Maybe Schopenhauer writes her material?

Mrs Hendy No . . . Burt Bacharach writes it.

Mr Hendy There's no 'S' in Burt Bacharach . . .

Mrs Hendy . . . Or in Hal David . . .

Mr Hendy Who's Hal David?

Mrs Hendy He writes the lyrics, Burt just writes the tunes . . .only now he's married to Carole Bayer Sager . . .

Mr Hendy Oh . . . Waiter . . . This conversation isn't very good.

Waiter Oh, I'm sorry, sir . . . We *do* have one today that's not on the menu. It's a sort of . . . er . . . speciality of the house. Live Organ Transplants.

Mrs Hendy Live Organ Transplants? What's *that*?

THE MEANING OF LIFE

PART V
LIVE ORGAN TRANSPLANTS

A photo of the Emperor Haile Selassie hangs on the wall of a suburban house. Upstairs 'Hava Nagila' is being played on a lone violin. The door bell rings.

Mr Bloke Don't worry dear, I'll get it!

> *He opens the door.*

Mr Bloke Yes?

First Man Hello, er can we have your liver . . .?

Mr Bloke My what?

First Man Your liver . . . it's a large glandular organ in your abdomen . . . you know it's a reddish-brown and it's sort of –

Mr Bloke Yes, I know what it is, but I'm using it.

Second Man Come on sir . . . don't muck us about.

> *They move in.*

Mr Bloke Hey!

> *They shut the door behind him.*
> *The first man makes a grab at his wallet and finds a card in it.*

First Man Hallo! What's this then . . .?

Mr Bloke A liver donor's card.

First Man Need we say more?

Second Man No.

Mr Bloke Look, I can't give it you now. It says 'In The Event of Death' . . .

First Man No one who has ever had their liver taken out by us has survived . . . .

> *The second man is rummaging around in a bag of clanking tools.*

Second Man Just lie there, sir. It won't take a minute.

> *They throw him onto the dining room table and, without any more ceremony, start to cut him open. A rather severe lady appears at the door.*

Mrs Bloke 'Ere, what's going on?

First Man He's donating his liver, madam . . .

Mr Bloke Aarrgh . . . oh! . . . aaargh ow! Ow!

Mrs Bloke Is this because he took out one of those silly cards?

First Man That's right, madam.

Mr Bloke Ow! Oooh! Oohh! Oh . . . oh . . . God . . . aargh aargh . . .

Mrs Bloke Typical of him. He goes down to the public library – sees a few signs up . . . comes home all full of good intentions. He gives blood . . . he does cold research . . . all that sort of thing.

Mr Bloke Aaaagh . . . oh . . . aaarghh!

Mrs Bloke What d'you do with them all anyway?

Second Man They all go to saving lives, madam.

Mr Bloke Aaaaargh! Oh . . . ow! Oh . . . oh my God!

Mrs Bloke That's what *he* used to say . . . it's all for the good of the country, he used to say.

Mr Bloke Aaaargh! . . . Ow! Ooh!

Mrs Bloke D'*you* think it's *all* for the good of the country?

First Man Uh?

Mrs Bloke D'*you* think it's *all* for the good of the country?

First Man Well I wouldn't know about that, madam . . . we're just doing our jobs, you know . . .

Mr Bloke Owwwwweeeeeeeeeh! Ow!

Mrs Bloke You're not doctors, then?

First Man Oh! . . . Blimey no . . .!

> *The second man grins and raises his eyes as he digs around in the stomach. They laugh.*
> *A head comes round the door . . . It's a young man.*

Young Man Mum, Dad, . . . I'm off out . . . now. I'll see you about seven. . . .

Mrs Bloke Righto, son . . . look after yourself.

Mr Bloke Aaargh . . . ow! Oh . . . aaargh aargh!

Mrs Bloke D'you er . . . fancy a cup of tea . . . ?

First Man Oh well, that would be very nice, yeah . . . . Thank you, thank you very much madam. Thank you. (*Aside.*) I thought she'd never ask . . .

> *She takes him into the kitchen and shuts the door. She bustles about preparing the tea . . .*

You do realise . . . he has to be . . . well . . . dead . . . by the terms of the card . . . before he donates his liver.

Mrs Bloke Well I told him that . . . but he never listens to me . . . silly man.

First Man Only . . . I was wondering what you was thinking of doing after that . . . I mean . . . will you stay on your own or . . . is there someone else . . . sort of . . . on the horizon . . . ?

Mrs Bloke I'm too old for that sort of thing. I'm past my prime . . .

First Man Not at all . . . you're a very attractive woman.

Mrs Bloke (*laughs a little*) Well . . . I'm certainly not thinking of getting hitched up again . . .

First Man Sure?

Mrs Bloke Sure.

First Man (*coming a little closer*) Can we have your liver then?

Mrs Bloke No . . . I don't want to die.

First Man Oh come on, it's perfectly natural. Only take a couple of minutes.

Mrs Bloke Oh . . . I'd be scared.

First Man All right, I'll tell you what. Look, listen to this –

> *A man in pink evening dress emerges from the fridge.*

Man in Pink Evening Dress Whenever life gets you down, Mrs Brown
> And things seem hard or tough
> And people are stupid obnoxious or daft
> And you feel that you've had quite enough . . .

As he starts to sing, the wall of the kitchen disintegrates to reveal a magnificent night sky. The vocalist in pink escorts Mrs Bloke up into the stars.

Just remember that you're standing on a planet that's
    evolving
And revolving at 900 miles an hour,
That's orbiting at 19 miles a second, so it's reckoned,
A sun that is the source of all our power.
The sun and you and me and all the stars that we can see,
Are moving at a million miles a day
In an outer spiral arm, at 40,000 miles an hour,
Of the galaxy we call the Milky Way.

Our galaxy itself contains 100 billion stars
It's 100,000 light years side to side.
It bulges in the middle, 16,000 light years thick
But out by us its just 3,000 light years wide
We're 30,000 light years from galactic central point,
We go round every 200 million years
And our galaxy is only one of millions of billions
In this amazing and expanding Universe.

The Universe itself keeps on expanding and expanding
In all of the directions it can whizz
As fast as it can go, at the speed of light you know,
12 million miles a minute, and that's the fastest speed there is.
So remember when you're feeling very small and insecure
How amazingly unlikely is your birth
And pray that there's intelligent life somewhere up in space
Because there's bugger all down here on earth.

The vocalist in pink climbs back into the fridge and the door slams to.

Mrs Bloke Makes you feel so sort of insignificant, doesn't it?

First Man Yeah yeah . . . Can we have your liver, then?

Mrs Bloke Yeah. All right, you talked me into it.

First Man Eric!

A lettering artist is just finishing painting the words 'Liver Donors Inc' onto a wall plaque enumerating all the subsidiaries of the Very Big Corporation of America.

Chairman (*of the Very Big Corporation of America*) . . . which brings us once again to the urgent realisation of just how much there is still left to own. Item 6 on the Agenda, the Meaning of Life . . . Now Harry, you've had some thoughts on this . . .

Harry That's right, yeah. I've had a team working on this over the past few weeks, and what we've come up with can be reduced to two fundamental concepts . . . . One . . . people are not wearing enough hats. Two . . . matter is energy; in the Universe there are many energy fields which we cannot normally perceive. Some energies have a spiritual source which act upon a person's soul. However, this soul does not exist *ab initio*, as orthodox Christianity teaches; it has to be brought into existence by a process of guided self-observation. However, this is rarely achieved owing to man's unique ability to be distracted from spiritual matters by everyday trivia.

    Pause.

Max What was that about hats again?

Harry Er . . . people aren't wearing enough.

Chairman Is this true?

Edmund (*who is sitting next to Harry*) Certainly. Hat sales have increased, but not *pari passu* . . . as our research –

Bert When you say 'enough', enough for what purpose . . .?

Gunther Can I ask with reference to your second point, when you say souls don't develop because people become distracted . . . has anyone noticed that building there before?

    They all turn towards the window to see a building approaching or sliding into position outside.

All Gulp! What? Good Lord!

The CRIMSON PERMANENT ASSURANCE

A tale of piracy
on the high seas
of finance

London, England

In the bleak days of 1983, as England languished in the doldrums of a ruinous monetarist policy, the good and loyal men of the Permanent Assurance Company – a once-proud family firm recently fallen on hard times – strained under the yoke of their oppressive new corporate management . . .

Pushed beyond the bounds of decent and reasonable victimisation — the aged retainers take their destiny in their own hands and . . . MUTINY!

And so – the Crimson Permanent Assurance was launched upon the high seas of international finance!

There it lay, the prize they sought – the richest jewel in the crown of the IMF – a financial district swollen with multi-nationals, conglomerates and fat, bloated merchant banks.

Hidden behind the faceless towering canyons of glass, the world of high finance sat smug and self-satisfied as their future, in the shape of their past, slipped silently through the streets – returning to wreak a terrible revenge.

Adopting, adapting, and improving traditional business practices the Permanent Assurance puts into motion an audacious and totally unsuspected Take-Over Bid.

And so, heartened by their initial success, the desperate and reasonably violent men of the Permanent Assurance battled on, until . . . as the sun set slowly in the west the outstanding return on their bold business venture became apparent. . . . The once proud financial giants lay in ruins – their assets stripped – their policies in tatters.

(*They Sing*)
It's fun to charter an accountant
And sail the wide accountan-cy,
To find, explore the funds offshore
And skirt the shoals of bankruptcy.

It can be manly in insurance:
We'll up your premium semi-annually,
It's all tax-deductible,
We're fairly incorruptible,
Sailing on the wide accountan-cy!

And so . . . they sailed off into the ledgers of history – one by one the financial capitals of the world crumbling under the might of their business acumen – or so it would have been . . . if certain modern theories concerning the shape of the world had not proved to be . . . disastrously wrong.

THE MEANING OF LIFE

PART VI
THE AUTUMN YEARS

Elegant restaurant. A man in a dressing gown, who is not Noël Coward sits at a piano.

Not Noël Coward Good evening ladies and gentlemen. Here's a little number I tossed off recently in the Caribbean. (*Sings*)

Isn't it awfully nice to have a penis,
Isn't it frightfully good to have a dong?
It's swell to have a stiffy,
It's divine to own a dick,
From the tiniest little tadger,
To the world's biggest prick.

So three cheers for your Willy or John Thomas,
Hooray for your one-eyed trouser snake,
Your piece of pork, your wife's best friend,
Your Percy or your cock,
You can wrap it up in ribbons,
You can slip it in your sock,
But don't take it out in public,
Or they will stick you in the dock,
And you won't come back.

Spontaneous applause breaks out all over the restaurant.

Oh . . . thank you very much.

Woman Oh what a frightfully witty song.

Clapping.

Mr Creosote enters.

First Fish (*in tank*) Oh shit! It's Mr Creosote.

All the fish disappear with six flicks of the tail.

Maitre D Ah good afternoon, sir, and how are we today?
Mr Creosote Better . . .

Maître D Better?
Mr Creosote Better get a bucket, I'm going to throw up.

Maître D Gaston! A bucket for monsieur!

They seat him at his usual table. A gleaming silver bucket is placed beside him and he leans over and throws up into it.

Maître D Merci Gaston.

He claps his hands and the bucket is whisked away.

Mr Creosote I haven't finished!

Maître D Oh! Pardon! Gaston! . . . A thousand pardons monsieur. (*Puts bucket back*)

The Maître D produces the menu as Mr Creosote continues spewing.

Maître D Now this afternoon we have monsieur's favourite – the jugged hare. The hare is *very* high, and the sauce is very rich with truffles, anchovies, Grand Marnier, bacon and cream.

Mr Creosote pauses. The Maître D claps his hands and signs to Gaston, who whisks away the bucket.

Maître D Thank you, Gaston.

Mr Creosote There's still more.

Gaston rapidly replaces the bucket.

Maître D Allow me! A new bucket for monsieur.

The Maître D picks the bucket up and hands it over to Gaston. Mr Creosote leans over and throws up onto the floor.
And the cleaning woman.
Gaston hurries off. The Maître D takes care to avoid the vomit and places the menu in front of Mr Creosote.

And maintenant, would monsieur care for an apéritif?

Creosote vomits over the menu. It is covered.

Or would you prefer to order straight away? Today we have for appetizers . . . er . . . excuse me . . .

The Maître D leans over and wipes away the sick with his hand so that the words of the menu are readable.

. . . moules marinières, pâté de foie gras, beluga caviar, eggs Benedictine, tarte de poireaux – that's leek tart – frogs' legs amandine or oeufs de caille Richard Shepherd – c'est à dire, little quails' eggs on a bed of puréed mushrooms, it's very delicate, very subtle . . .

Mr Creosote I'll have the lot.

Maître D A wise choice, monsieur! And now, how would you like it served? All mixed up in a bucket?

Mr Creosote Yes. With the eggs on top.

Maître D But of course, avec les oeufs frites.

Mr Creosote And don't skimp on the pâté.

Maître D Oh monsieur I can assure you, just because it is mixed up with all the other things we would not dream of giving you less than the full amount. In fact I will personally make sure you have a *double* helping. Maintenant quelque chose à boire – something to drink, monsieur?

Mr Creosote Yeah, six bottles of Château Latour '45 and a double Jeroboam of champagne.

Maître D Bon, and the usual brown ales . . .?

Mr Creosote Yeah . . . No wait a minute . . . I think I could only manage six crates today.

Maître D Tut tut tut! I hope monsieur was not overdoing it last night . . .?

Mr Creosote Shut up!

Maître D D'accord. Ah the new bucket and the cleaning woman.

Gaston arrives. The Cleaning Woman gets down on her hands and knees. Mr Creosote vomits over her.

Some guests at another table start to leave. The Maître D approaches.

Maître D Monsieur, is there something wrong with the food?

The Maître D indicates the table of half-eaten main courses. The guests shrink from his vomit-covered hand. The Maître D realises and shakes a little off. It hits another guest, who wipes his eye.

Guest No. The food was . . . excellent . . .

Maître D Perhaps you are not happy with the service?

Guest Er no . . . no . . . no complaints.

Guest's Wife It's just we have to go – um – I'm having rather a heavy period.

A slight embarrassed silence while the rest of the party look at her.

Guest And . . . we . . . have a train to catch.

Guest's Wife (*as if covering her previous gaffe*) Oh! Yes! Yes . . . of course! We have a train to catch . . . and I don't want to start bleeding over the seats.

An awkward pause. The Maître D gropes for words.

Guest Perhaps we should be going . . .

They start to go. The Maître D follows.

Maître D Very well, monsieur. Thank you so much, so nice to see you and I hope very much we will see you again very soon. Au revoir, monsieur.

He pauses. A look of awful realization suffuses his face.

Maître D . . . Oh dear . . . I've trodden in monsieur's bucket.

The Maître D claps his hands.

Another bucket for monsieur . . .

Mr Creosote is sick down the Maître D's trousers.

and perhaps a hose . . .

Someone at another table gently throws up.

Companion Oh Max, really!

At another table someone else has really thrown up all over the place. His mother and brother look at him incredulously. Meanwhile Mr Creosote has scoffed the lot. The Maître D approaches him with a silver tray.

Maître D And finally, monsieur, a wafer-thin mint.

Mr Creosote No.

Maître D Oh sir! It's only a tiny little thin one.

Mr Creosote No. Fuck off – I'm full . . . (*Belches*)

Maître D Oh sir . . . it's only *wafer* thin.

Mr Creosote Look – I couldn't eat another thing. I'm absolutely stuffed. Bugger off.

Maître D Oh sir, just . . . just *one* . . .

Mr Creosote Oh all right. Just one.

Maître D Just the one, sir . . . voilà . . . bon appétit . . .

Mr Creosote somehow manages to stuff the wafer-thin mint into his mouth and then swallows. The Maître D takes a flying leap and cowers behind some potted plants. There is an ominous splitting sound. Mr Creosote looks rather helpless and then he explodes, covering waiters, diners and technicians in a truly horrendous mix of half digested food, entrails and parts of his body. People start vomiting.

Maître D (*returns to Mr Creosote's table*) Thank you, sir, and now the check.

THE MEANING OF LIFE

PART VI B
THE MEANING OF LIFE

Some time later.
The Cleaning Woman is still on her knees, cleaning up the remains of Mr Creosote. The Maître D
lights up a cigarette in pensive mood.

Maître D You know, Maria, I sometimes wonder whether we'll ever discover the meaning of it all
working in a place like this.

Maria (shrugs) Oh, I've worked in worse places . . . philosophically speaking.

Maître D Really, Maria?

Maria Yes . . . I used to work in the Académie Française
But it didn't do me any good at all . . .
And I once worked in the library in the Prado in Madrid,
But it didn't teach me nothing, I recall . . .
And the Library of Congress you'd have thought would hold some key . . .
But it didn't. And neither did the Bodleian Library.
In the British Museum I hoped to find some clue,
I worked there from 9 till 6 – read every volume through,
But it didn't teach me nothing about Life's mystery . . .
I just kept getting older, and it got more difficult to see.
Until eventually me eyes went and me arthritis got bad,
And so now I'm cleaning up in here – but I can't really be sad,
Cause you see I feel that Life's a game
You sometimes win or lose,
And though I may be down right now
At least I don't work for Jews . . .

　　　The Maître D pours the bucket over her head and turns to the camera looking most
　　　upset.

Maître D I'm so sorry . . . I had no idea we had a racist working here . . . I apologise . . . most sincerely . . . I mean . . . where are you going – I can explain . . . oh, quel dommage . . .

The camera pans off the Maître D and alights on Gaston, smoking a cigarette.

Gaston As for me . . . if you want to know what I think . . . I'll show you something . . . come with me . . .

Maître D (*out of shot*) I was saying that – hallo . . . hallo . . .

Gaston Come on . . . this way.

He nods to the camera and walks out of the restaurant and the camera follows him.

Voice of Maître D I can explain everything.

Gaston Come on – don't be shy. Mind the stairs . . . . All right. I think this will help explain.

He walks through the town.

Gaston Come along. . . . Come along . . . . Over here . . . . Come on . . . . Come on . . . This way. . . . Come on. . . . Stay by me, uh? Nearly there now.

Eventually Gaston comes over a hill and nods down to a little thatched cottage nestling idyllically in a valley. Smoke rises up from the chimney.

You see that? That's where I was born. You know, one day, when I was a little boy, my mother she took me on her knee and she said: 'Gaston, my son. The world is a beautiful place. You must go into it, and love everyone, not hate people. You must try and make everyone happy, and bring peace and contentment everywhere you go'. And so . . . I became a waiter . . .

There is a rather long pause, while he looks a bit self-deprecating and nods shyly at the camera.

Well . . . it's . . . it's not much of a philosophy, I know . . . but . . . well . . . fuck you . . . I can live my own life in my own way if I want to. Fuck off! Don't come following me!

THE MEANING OF LIFE

PART VII
DEATH

Distraught Male Voice I just can't go on. I'm no good any more, goodbye . . . goodbye . . . aaaargh! . . . Aaaargh!

A leaf falls to the ground.

Distraught Female Voice Oh my God! What'll I do!? I can't live without him . . . I . . . aaaargh!

Another leaf falls.

Distraught Children's Voices Mummy . . . Mummy . . . Mummy . . . Daddy . . .

Two more leaves fall.

More Distraught Voices Oh no! Aaaargh!

All the remaining leaves fall with one accord.

This man is about to die. In a few moments now he will be killed. For Arthur Jarrett is a convicted criminal who has been allowed to choose the manner of his own execution.

Governor Arthur Charles Herbert Runcie MacAdam Jarrett, you have been convicted by twelve good persons and true, of the crime of first degree making of gratuitous sexist jokes in a moving picture.

Padre Ashes to ashes, dust to dust . . .

Ingmar Bergman now takes over the direction of the film and re-invokes one of his greatest triumphs on a low budget. Bare windswept trees starkly silhouetted against the . . . oh you know. Lots of good sound effects, too: howling wind, howling dogs, howling sabre-toothed field mice. Suddenly we see the Grim Reaper. He is hooded, in a black cloak with a sackcloth jock-strap, and bearing . . . a scythe.

He materializes outside a lowly cottage and strikes the door with his scythe. Geoffrey, who is Marketing Director of Uro-Pacific Ltd, opens the door. From inside the house come the sounds of a dinner party.

Geoffrey Yes?

 Pause. The Reaper breathes death-rattlingly.

 Is it about the hedge?

 More breathing.

 Look, I'm awfully sorry but . . .

Grim Reaper I am the Grim Reaper.

Geoffrey Who?

Grim Reaper The Grim Reaper.

Geoffrey Yes I see . . .

Grim Reaper I am Death.

Geoffrey Yes well, the thing is, we've got some people from America for dinner tonight . . .

 Geoffrey's wife, Angela is coming to see who is at the door. She calls:

Angela Who is it, darling?

Geoffrey It's a Mr Death or something . . . he's come about the reaping . . . (*To Reaper.*) I don't think we need any at the moment.

Angela (*appearing*) Hallo. Well don't leave him hanging around outside darling, ask him in.

Geoffrey Darling, I don't think it's quite the moment . . .

Angela Do come in, come along in, come and have a drink, do. Come on . . .

 She returns to her guests.

It's one of the little men from the village . . . . Do come in, please. This is Howard Katzenberg from Philadelphia. . . .

Katzenberg Hi.

Angela And his wife, Debbie.

Debbie Hallo there.

Angela And these are the Portland-Smythes, Jeremy and Fiona.

Fiona Good evening.

Angela This is Mr Death.

> *There is a slightly awkward pause.*

Well do get Mr Death a drink, darling.

> *The Grim Reaper looks a little startled.*

Angela Mr Death is a reaper.

Grim Reaper The Grim Reaper.

Angela Hardly surprising in this weather, ha ha ha . . .

Katzenberg So you still reap around here do you, Mr Death?

Grim Reaper I am the Grim Reaper.

Geoffrey (*sotto voce*) That's about all he says . . . (*Loudly*) There's your drink, Mr Death.

Angela Do sit down.

Debbie We were just talking about some of the awful problems facing the –

> *The Grim Reaper knocks the glass off the table. Startled silence.*

Angela Would you prefer white? I'm afraid we don't have any beer.

Jeremy The Stilton's awfully good.

Grim Reaper I am not of this world.

> *He walks into the middle of the table. There is a sharp intake of breath all round.*

Geoffrey Good Lord!

> *The penny is beginning to drop.*

Grim Reaper I am Death.

Debbie (*nervously*) Well isn't that extraordinary? We were just talking about death only five minutes ago.

Angela (*even more nervously*) Yes we were. You know, whether death is really . . . the end . . .

Debbie As my husband, Howard here, feels . . . or whether there is . . . and one so hates to use words like 'soul' or 'spirit' . . .

Jeremy But what *other* words can one use . . .

Geoffrey Exactly . . .

Grim Reaper You do not understand.

Debbie Ah no . . . obviously not. . . .

Katzenberg Let me tell you something, Mr Death . . .

Grim Reaper You do not understand!

Katzenberg Just one moment. I would like to express on behalf of everyone here, what a really unique experience this is . . .

Jeremy Hear hear.

Angela Yes, we're *so* delighted that you dropped in, Mr Death . . .

Katzenberg Can I just finish please . . .

Debbie Mr Death . . . is there an after-life?

Katzenberg Dear, if you could just wait please a moment . . .

Angela Are you sure you wouldn't like some sherry?

Katzenberg Angela, I'd like just to say this at this time . . .

Grim Reaper Be quiet!

Katzenberg Can I just say this at this time, please . . .

Grim Reaper Silence!!! I have come for you.

Pause as this sinks in. Sidelong glances. A stifled fart.

Angela . . . You mean to . . .

Grim Reaper . . . Take you away. That is my purpose. I am Death.

Geoffrey Well that's cast rather a gloom over the evening hasn't it?

Katzenberg I don't see it that way, Geoff. Let me tell you what I think we're dealing with here, a potentially positive learning experience . . .

Grim Reaper Shut up! Shut up you American. You always talk, you Americans, you talk and you talk and say 'Let me tell you something' and 'I just wanna say this'. Well you're dead now, so shut up.

Katzenberg Dead?

Grim Reaper Dead.

Angela All of us??

Grim Reaper All of you.

Geoffrey Now look here. You barge in here, quite uninvited, break glasses and then announce quite casually that we're all dead. Well I would remind you that you are a guest in this house and . . .

The Grim Reaper pokes him in the eye.

Grim Reaper Be quiet! You Englishmen . . . You're all so fucking pompous and none of you have got any balls.

Debbie Can I ask you a question?

Grim Reaper What?

Debbie . . . How can we all have died at the *same* time?

Grim Reaper (*pointing*) The salmon mousse! (*They all goggle.*)

Geoffrey (*to Angela*) Darling, you didn't use tinned salmon did you?

Angela (*unbelievably embarrassed*) I'm most dreadfully embarrassed . . .

Grim Reaper Now, the time has come. Follow . . . follow me . . .

>   Geoffrey suddenly runs forward with a revolver. He looses four shots at the Grim Reaper
>   from about three feet. They pass through him. Pause. Everyone is rather embarrassed.

Geoffrey Sorry . . . . Just . . . testing . . . . Sorry . . . (*He sits*)

Grim Reaper Follow me. *Now*! (*They suddenly die, slumping forward. The candles gutter and go out.*)

Grim Reaper Come! (*Out of their bodies, spirit forms arise and follow the Grim Reaper*).

Angela The fishmonger promised me he'd have some fresh salmon and he's normally *so* reliable . . .

Jeremy Can we bring our glasses?

Fiona Good idea.

Debbie Hey I didn't even eat the mousse . . . (*They follow the Grim Reaper out of the house.*)

Angela Honestly, darling, I'm so embarrassed . . . . I mean to serve salmon with botulism at a dinner party is social death . . .

Jeremy Shall we take our cars?

Geoffrey Why not?

>   Slightly to the Grim Reaper's surprise, they follow him up to heaven in a Porsche, a
>   Jensen and a Volvo.

Grim Reaper Behold . . . Paradise!

Heaven bears a striking resemblance to a Holiday Inn.

Mr Hendy I love it here, darling.

Mrs Hendy Me too, Marvin.

Receptionist Hello. Welcome to Heaven. Excuse me, could you just sign here, please sir? Thank you. There's a table for you through there in the restaurant. For the ladies . . .

Fiona (*reading the box of chocolates that has been handed to her*) 'After Life Mints'.

Receptionist Happy Christmas.

Debbie Oh is it Christmas today?

Receptionist Of course madam, it's Christmas *every* day, in Heaven.

Debbie How about that?

   A restaurant in Heaven. It is full of all the characters who have died in the film. Plus some of the naked girls, because . . . well, we don't have to give a reason, do we?

Tony Bennett Good evening ladies and gentlemen, it's truly a real honourable experience to be here this evening a very wonderful and emotional moment for all of us, and I'd like to sing a song for all of you: (*sings*) It's Christmas in Heaven: all the children sing

It's Christmas in Heaven
Hark hark those church bells ring'

It's Christmas in Heaven
The snow falls from the sky . . .

But it's nice and warm and everyone
Looks smart and wears a tie

It's Christmas in Heaven
There's great films on TV . . .
'The Sound of Music' *twice* an hour
And 'Jaws' I, II *and* III

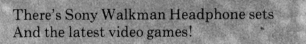

There's gifts for all the family
There's toiletries and trains . . .

There's Sony Walkman Headphone sets
And the latest video games!

It's Christmas It's Christmas in Heaven
Hip hip hip hip hip hooray
Every single day
Is Christmas Day!

It's Christmas It's Christmas in Heaven
Hip hip hip hip hip hooray
Every single day
Is Christmas Day!'

But before we get to the end of this chorus the TV set is switched off and the whole picture collapses into a little spot and we pull out to find that we have been watching a TV set in front of the Middle of the Film lady.

Lady Presenter (*briskly*) Well, that's the End of the Film, now here's the Meaning of Life.

An envelope is handed to her. She opens it in a business-like way.

Thank you Brigitte. (*She reads.*) . . . Well, it's nothing very special. Try and be nice to people, avoid eating fat, read a good book every now and then, get some walking in and try and live together in peace and harmony with people of all creeds and nations. And finally, here are some completely gratuitous pictures of penises to annoy the censors and to hopefully spark some sort of controversy which it seems is the only way these days to get the jaded video-sated public off their fucking arses and back in the sodding cinema. Family entertainment bollocks! What they want is filth, people doing things to each other with chainsaws during tupperware parties, babysitters being stabbed with knitting needles by gay presidential candidates, vigilante groups strangling chickens, armed bands of theatre critics exterminating mutant goats – where's the fun in pictures? Oh well, there we are – here's the theme music. Goodnight.

THE MEANING OF LIFE

First Fish	Graham Chapman
Second Fish	John Cleese
Third Fish	Terry Gilliam
Fourth Fish	Eric Idle
Fifth Fish	Terry Jones
Sixth Fish	Michael Palin
Creosotish Man	George Silver
Singer –	
'Meaning of Life'	Eric Idle
Mrs Moore	Valerie Whittington
First Nurse	Judy Loe
Second Nurse	Imogen Bickford Smith
First Doctor	Graham Chapman
Second Doctor	John Cleese
Mr Moore	Eric Idle
Administrator	Michael Palin
Dad	Michael Palin
Mum	Terry Jones
Priest	Terry Jones
Bride	Jennifer Franks
Groom	Andrew Maclachlan
Mr Blackitt	Graham Chapman
Mrs Blackitt	Eric Idle
Martin Luther	Terry Jones
Hymie	Michael Palin
Mamie	Graham Chapman
Daughters	Victoria Plum
	Anne Rosenfeld
Headmaster	John Cleese
Chaplain	Michael Palin
Wymer	Graham Chapman
Biggs	Terry Jones
Carter	Michael Palin
Watson	Eric Idle
Mrs Williams	Patricia Quinn
Captain Biggs	Terry Jones
Blackitt	Eric Idle
Spadger	Michael Palin
Walters	Terry Gilliam
Sturridge	John Cleese
Hordern	Graham Chapman
General	Graham Chapman
R.S.M.	Michael Palin
Atkinson	Eric Idle
Coles	Graham Chapman
Wycliff	Andrew Maclachlan
Pakenham Walsh	Michael Palin
Ainsworth	John Cleese
Chadwick	Simon Jones
Perkins	Eric Idle
Livingstone	Graham Chapman
Sergeant	Terry Jones
Another Cheery	
Cockney	Andrew Maclachlan
A Severed Head	Mark Holmes
Another Terrible	
Casualty	Eric Idle

Front End	Eric Idle
Rear End	Michael Palin
Zulu Announcer	Terry Gilliam
Lady Presenter	Michael Palin
Man with	
Bendy Arms	Terry Jones
Woman	Graham Chapman
Troll with a Tray	Mark Holmes
Mr Hendy	Michael Palin
Mrs Hendy	Eric Idle
Joeline	Terry Gilliam
Waitress	Carol Cleveland
Waiter	John Cleese
Mr Bloke	Terry Gilliam
First Man	John Cleese
Second Man	Graham Chapman
Mrs Bloke	Terry Jones
Young Man	Peter Løvstrom
Distinguished	
Vocalist in Pink	Eric Idle
Noël Coward*	Eric Idle
Mr Creosote	Terry Jones
Maitre D	John Cleese
Gaston	Eric Idle
First Guest	Graham Chapman
Second Guest	Mark Holmes
First Guest's Wife	Carol Cleveland
Second Guest's	
Wife	Angela Mann
Third Guest	Andrew Maclachlan
Cleaning Woman	Terry Jones
Governor	Michael Palin
Arthur Jarrett	Graham Chapman
Padre	Michael Palin
Grim Reaper	John Cleese
Geoffrey	Graham Chapman
Angela	Eric Idle
Jeremy	Simon Jones
Fiona	Terry Jones
Katzenberg	Terry Gilliam
Debbie	Michael Palin
Receptionist	Carol Cleveland
Tony Bennett**	Graham Chapman

*Not *the* Noël Coward, of course
**Not *the* Tony Bennett, of course

Photographed by	Peter Hannan B.S.C.
Edited by	Julian Doyle
Production Designer	Harry Lange
Costume Designer	Jim Acheson
Choreography	Arlene Phillips
Makeup and Hair Design	Maggie Weston
Special Effects Supervisor	George Gibbs

Starred

Sydney Arnold	Cameron Miller
Ross Davidson	Paddy Ryan
Eric Francis	Eric Stovell
Russell Kilminster	Andrew Bicknell
Peter Merrill	Tim Doublas
Larry Noble	Billy John
John Scott Martin	Len Marten
Guy Bertrand	Gareth Milne
Myrtle Devenish	Leslie Sarony
Matt Frewer	Wally Thomas
Peter Mantle	

Director of Photography	Roger Pratt
Art Director	John Beard
Make-up Artist	Elaine Carew
Hairdressers	Maureen Stephenson
	Sallie Evans
Wardrobe	Joyce Stoneman
Music	John Du Prez

First published in Great Britain in 1983
by Methuen London Ltd
11 New Fetter Lane, London EC4P 4EE

Copyright © 1983 The Monty Python Partnership

ISBN 0 413 53380 8

Made and printed in Great Britain by
Redwood Burn Ltd,
Trowbridge, Wiltshire

AY THE ANGRY ZULUS
LACKED JOHN CLEESE!

rising hits
ython epic

By SUN REPORTER

ZANY comic John Cleese faced a new Zulu uprising yesterday . . . in the hills of south west Scotland.

Angry hordes of black extras "downed spears" during filming of a new Monty Python epic near Glasgow.

Four bus-loads of coloured students had signed on at £24 a day to re-enact the famous Battle of Rorke's Drift for the film The Meaning Of Life.

But they baulked when they arrived at Strathblane and were told to get into tribal costume.

The 120 black warriors went straight on strike — leaving just 30 Asians to represent a ferocious African nation.

As they headed back for Glasgow, the rebel extras said they thought they were making an educational film.

They slammed their tribal roles as "an insult."

The whole episode was like a sketch dreamed up by the Python team. And there was more silliness to follow.

Director Terry Jones decided to carry on regardless . . . with actors playing the bold Welsh troops outnumbering the warriors by three to one.

But as filming finally began the heavens opened.

Recruit

And long-legged Cleese leaped about among the extras demanding: "Which of you bastards did a rain dance?"

Last night, producer John Goldstone was desperately trying to recruit more Zulus.

They advertised for 150 extras in shops, universities and community centres . . . and soon discovered there were not many Zulus in Glasgow.

ZULU! of the de...

The Editor
The Sun
30 Bouverie Street
London EC4

Dear Sir,

I am afraid I have to write to you again to complain! I hope this will not become a habit.

You wrote a story on Friday about a rather funny situation that arose during the Monty Python filming in Scotland last week which you got pretty right.

However, in paragraph 3 from the end of the story, you say "And long-legged Cleese leaped about among the extras demanding :'Which of you bastards did a rain dance?'"

Now this is a total invention of your writer. I never mentioned the words "rain dance" nor did the thought cross my mind. Neither did I "leap about"; nor refer to the extras as "bastards".

So, the first grounds for my complaint are that the paragraph is completely untrue. The second ground for complaint is that, in the UK where there are racial tensions, it does not help my career to have attributed to me a remark which a lot of people would feel was racialist.

I know what happened. I am a zany madcap comic and your writer thought of the joke and decided to attribute it to me. It may be a minor matter but I do think it is quite unprofessional.

I do hope you agree.

Yours faithfully,

John Cleese

John Cleese

THE Sun

Registered No. 679215 England
Telex: ... 267827
Telephone 01-353 3030

Registered Office:
30 Bouverie Street, Fleet Street, London, EC4 8DE

29th September, 1982.

John Cleese, Esq.,
&, ...
London W1 3AA.

Dear Mr. Cleese,

I regret the delay in answering your letter which I found on my return from holiday. Your suggestion for a contest certainly has merit but is not really practicable.

Our correspondent still claims that the words were said as he reported them, and you insist that you were not the speaker. The young man is reliable and there seems no chance of reconciliation. His reporting has not been under fire previously.

The remarks were reported to voice the frustration which the weather was causing.

Perhaps you will let me know of any other original ideas that might help us to come to an amicable solution.

Best wishes,

Yours sincerely,

Kenneth Donlan
Managing Editor

---

6 October 1982

Dear Mr Donlan,

Thank you for your letter.

Chicken!

You ask me for another idea to resolve the problem. Well, the problem is, put bluntly, that your correspondent is lying through his teeth (extremely uncomfortable position).

Now, as I have said, I have sixty odd witnesses. How can I use them to convince you? Shall I ask them to write individually, or would a list of signatures on one letter suffice?

I do hope, like you, that we can settle this amicably.

Best wishes,

John Cleese

John Cleese

PS I hope you have no objection to our including this correspondence in the Monty Python book of the film.

PPS A correspondent of mine tells me you were recently seen running stark naked down Fleet Street shouting "Enoch Powell has a glass leg". Is my correspondent by any chance distorting the facts?